INSPIRED GARDENING

Discovering the Heart of God While in the Garden

Susan Elane Berry

Text copyright 2016 by Susan Elane Berry. All rights reserved. All of the poems and stories in this work are original and do not infringe upon the legal rights of any other person or work. No part of this book may be reproduced or transmitted in any form or by any means, electronic or mechanical, including photography, recording, or any information storage and retrieval system, without permission in writing from the publisher. The only exceptions are brief excerpts and reviews.

Author and Publisher: Susan Elane Berry

Editor: Scott Lyons

Scripture taken from the New King James Version®. Copyright ©1982 by Thomas Nelson. Used by permission. All rights reserved.

The "NIV" and "The New International Version" trademarks are registered in the United States Patent and Trademark Office by International Bible Society. Use of either trademark requires the permission of International Bible Society.

ISBN #978-0-99060607-4-1

Printed in the United States

Acknowledgements

This book is truly a love letter to God. The devotionals herein have brought me love, freedom, healing, and understanding. But first and foremost they have brought me closer to the heart of Father God, the great I Am. My passion and love for gardening was a seed that God placed in me when he formed me in my mother's womb. In his wisdom, the seed did not germinate into a talent until the age of forty-three. Without his guidance, open doors, and divine path, I would not have been able to publish my first book. From the seed of a green thumb has sprouted a writer and an author. God's plan is miraculous, surprising, and exciting! Thank you, Father, for blessing me with talents that can bless others.

My husband, Don, is a dedicated, patient man. He is also an encourager. He has been my best friend and partner in this homestead adventure, and without his encouragement I would never have gone to college at age fifty for a degree in horticulture. Thank you, Don, for your confidence in me. Thank you for your patience with me when I changed the garden plan thirty-seven times. Thank you for the blessing of you and your tools when I came to you with a picture of a chicken coop in my hands. But most of all, Don, thank you for loving God and following Jesus with me. I love you endlessly.

Thank you to Scott, my editor. Without your expertise, patience, and easy-to-understand guidance, the goal of being a published author would have been daunting and overwhelming.

Introduction

"I come to the garden alone,
While the dew is still on the roses,
And the voice I hear falling on my ear,
The Son of God discloses."
— C. Austin Miles, *"In the Garden"*

The Bible often speaks of gardening, sowing, cultivating, harvesting, and even weeding. God decided to begin the human race in a garden; he must have wanted us to spend some time there.

As I journey through a year in my garden, I see the many seasons of my life and God's plan unfolding, manifesting his destiny for me. In my garden I receive simple joys and profound revelations. Creation surges through the soil; creativity germinates from each seed; and revelation is the harvest that feeds my heart, mind, soul, and spirit. Each time I walk with the Lord in between the rows of plants, I am newly awakened. Working in the soil on my knees is not a chore, but an opportunity to commune with my Father and thank him for everything with which he has blessed me.

Everyone needs a place where they can go to have more intimate times with God. The mountains speak majestically to some during their retreats with the Lord. For others, the ocean breezes and rhythmic ebbing of the tides make the whispers of the Father's heart clearer. For me, I find my deeper, more intimate moments with God in the garden. As I walk through a section of tall corn, feeling the long wispy leaves brush over me as I pass by, I sense a gentleness and quietness that stills my soul and opens my ears to his voice.

God provides so much for us through gardening. He offers us peace, sustenance, beauty, and wonder as we witness all the life and fruitfulness that happens there.

As I share my encounters and wonder with you in this devotional, I hope you will see the enduring promises in your own garden and hear God beckoning, "Come, let me show you my heart as we tend this garden together."

"Then the Lord God took the man and put him in the garden of Eden to tend and keep it."
—*Genesis 2:15 (NKJV)*

Table of Contents

Devotion One
    God's Devine Math of One Seed 11
    Favorite Recipe: Simple Squash Pie 14

Devotion Two
    Growing Together. 17
    Favorite Recipe: Creamed Peas and 21
       New Potatoes

Devotion Three
    The Depth of Our Roots 23
    Compost 27

Devotion Four
    Peas in a Pod: The Joy of Growing Together . . 29
    Favorite Recipe: Peas and Mushrooms. 33

Devotion Five
    Growing in the Winter of Our Life. 35
    Favorite Recipe: Spinach and Pear Salad 39

Devotion Six
    Do You Need to Be Fertilized? 41

Devotion Seven
    Finding Our Place. 45
    Favorite Recipe: Artichoke Stuffing Mix. 48

Devotion Eight
    Some Things Just Take Time. 51
    Favorite Recipe: Roasted Asparagus 55

Devotion Nine
    God Wants to Compost You 57

Devotion Ten
    Be What You Were Created to Be 63

Devotion Eleven
    Patience and Winter Squash 67
    Favorite Recipe: Winter Squash Rolls 71

Devotion Twelve
    Indeterminate Blessings 73
    Favorite Recipe: Too-Many-Tomatoes Salsa. . . 77

Devotion Thirteen
    Sharing and Imparting Your Gifts 79
    Inspiration in the Garden and the Kitchen. . . . 84

More of Susan's Favorite Recipes
    Broccoli Cheddar Cheese Soup. 86
    Beet Salad 87
    Zucchini Brownies 88

About the Author. 95

Growing Tip

Musquee de Provence is similar to other winter squash and pumpkins in that they like lots of space to roam. Plant where you have space for them to vine and spread out. Due to the size of these squash, it is not recommended to trellis them. Place a plate or pie plate upside down (so as not to collect water) under each squash as it grows to keep it off the ground. This helps prevent rot as well as insects from boring into the squash. Plant Musquee de Provence in full sun and feed every four weeks or so with an organic vegetable fertilizer—such as a granular, slow-release type of fertilizer or a liquid, water-soluble seaweed and fish emulsion. Sow the seeds in loose soil that is rich in organic matter and aged manure. You do not need to fertilize for the first four to six weeks, as the rich soil will feed the plants in the beginning. Fertilize the squash when blooms begin to appear. Do not fertilize in the final four weeks of growth. These squash require about 120 days of growing time, so plant accordingly. They do not hold up well when temperatures go much below 40°F.

Devotion One

God's Devine Math of One Seed

When God created the first garden, he was obviously planning ahead. After thirteen years of raising my own produce crops, I am still amazed that a seed can become sustenance. As I hold a single seed in between my fingers and walk down a row of my garden, I wonder at this hard shell that is no bigger than my pinky fingernail, knowing God has placed his creative energy and power inside of it. Creation sleeps within the seed coat. And as each participant in this perfect design plays its part, a miracle takes place—the miracle of life and propagation.

One of my favorite vegetables to grow is winter squash. I love the foods of my native New England, and one of the most popular is the butternut squash. For many years I only grew butternut squash as my winter squash crop. Rich in color and flavor, and firm in texture, it is an all-around good squash that holds well in dry storage and freezes well after being cooked.

Last year, at the encouragement of a gardening friend, I decided to try another winter squash variety. Sometimes called the Cinderella pumpkin because of its deeply lobed shape, the Musquee de Provence, a French heirloom originating in the South of France, is a variety of the *Cucurbita moschata* species of squash and pumpkin. Introduced in the United States in 1899 by Vaughan's Seed Store of Chicago, this pumpkin has become a new favorite winter squash for me to grow in my garden.

God promises to provide for all our needs. As we sow, he is faithful to bless the seed and multiply it. One seed in the hand of our heavenly Father becomes a blessing not once, but over and over. And he creates it to serve more than its original purpose and bless more than its original steward. To my amazement, his promise of abundance was revealed to me through the Musquee de Provence squash. You may think a single squash seed will produce a squash, and it will—and that in itself would be a tremendous blessing. But it does so much more.

One Musquee de Provence seed will grow one plant. From that one plant, the sower can harvest three or four squash weighing twenty pounds or more. One of my plants produced three squash each over twenty pounds. One of these weighed twenty-nine pounds. It had two pounds of peel that I used in my garden as compost. One and a half pounds of seed pulp were removed and fed to my flock of hens. The seeds that were removed, cleaned and dried to be planted back into my garden and given to others for their gardens totaled 467 seeds. Nearly every seed that germinated for me produced three squash, each large enough to make ten to fifteen pounds of cooked squash. My husband and I will both eat about a half pound of squash at a meal. So from this single, twenty-nine pound squash we could get around 1,400 more squash harvested from the 467 seeds. If the 1,400 squash weighed an average of fifteen pounds—minus four pounds each in peel, seed, and pulp—they could produce 15,400 pounds of edible squash. If one half pound of cooked squash is eaten per

adult, those 467 seeds could feed 7,700 people. Divine math. One seed sown in faith.

As we sow into the Kingdom for God's glory, we are planting for God. He is faithful to water, cultivate, and bring forth an abundant harvest from one seed, sown in generosity and faith. What kind of seed has God given you and asked you to sow? On bended knee, with hands in the soil, sow your seed and watch God's divine math multiply it to bless you and countless others. He is faithful to give an increase for you to share. In turn, others can sow and harvest even more seed, and so on forever, to his glory. One seed in our hand provides us with a harvest, but one seed in his hand can provide a miraculous abundance.

> *"But this I say: He who sows sparingly will also reap sparingly, and he who sows bountifully will also reap bountifully. So let each one give as he purposes in his heart, not grudgingly or of necessity; for God loves a cheerful giver. And God is able to make all grace abound toward you, that you, always having all sufficiency in all things, may have an abundance for every good work. As it is written: "He has dispersed abroad, He has given to the poor; His righteousness endures forever." Now may He who supplies seed to the sower, and bread for food, supply and multiply the seed you have sown and increase the fruits of your righteousness, while you are enriched in everything for all liberality, which causes thanksgiving through us to God."*
>
> —*2 Corinthians 9:6–11 (NKJV)*

Favorite Recipe

SIMPLE SQUASH PIE

2 cups squash puree*
2 eggs
1 can sweetened condensed milk
1/4 cup hot water
1 teaspoon cinnamon
1/2 teaspoon ground ginger
1/2 teaspoon ground nutmeg
1/4 teaspoon ground cloves
1 deep dish pie crust

In a large bowl, stir or whisk together all filling ingredients. Pour into pie crust and bake at 350°F for 40 to 50 minutes or until the center of the pie is set and the edge of the crust is golden brown. Cool, and serve either at room temperature or chilled.

Makes 8–10 servings.

*This squash holds a lot of water and is best cut into sections and baked on a cookie sheet in an oven until tender. Remove the squash meat from the shell and mash in a large bowl. Transfer mashed squash to a colander and allow it to drain for an hour or more, occasionally pressing gently to remove all the liquid. The puree can be used immediately or frozen in freezer bags for future use.

Notes

Notes

INSPIRED GARDENING

Growing Tip

When sowing companion plants, be sure to allow plenty of growing space for each of the plants. Plants thrive when planted close together—through water retention and the prevention of weeds—but keep in mind that plants also need good air circulation. So don't overcrowd by planting species of similar height too close. Instead, plant shorter plants next to taller ones. For example, basil plants do well planted near taller tomato plants. They're great together—especially on homemade pizza!

Devotion Two

Growing Together

During my pursuit of organic gardening, I discovered the practice of companion planting. The purpose of this method of planting is for different varieties of plants to assist one another with the factors necessary for the productivity of the crop. Certain plants or crops are partnered with completely different varieties that are beneficial to their neighbors.

Companion plants help each other grow and use garden space efficiently. For example, vining plants such as cucumbers can be grown on an A-frame trellis in the heat of summer over a raised bed to allow shade-loving lettuce to grow happily underneath. Companions prevent pest problems: When planted next to cucumbers or squash, nasturtiums repel cucumber beetles and squash bugs. Companions improve and stimulate the growth of other plants, as marjoram does for most vegetables.

Companions Who Prevent Pest Problems

Onions and garlic planted next to just about anything will repel insects. Now I have had "onion and garlic" acquaintances over the years at church that just didn't fit in with my personality. I remember one person, for example, who I felt awkward around. I would end up in the same Bible class with this person, or we would bump into each other at the weekly prayer meeting or Ladies' fellowship. I found myself worrying whether she was going to be at these events. I didn't know what to do with her. My mind and soul were apprehensive, but what was happening in my spirit was surprising: If she were the one to pray the opening prayer or share a testimony, it would be a blessing to me. I was touched by her genuineness. Her love was apparent, and her discernment enlightening. She repelled the enemy, and her power in prayer was invigorating. There were those times I would have to drag myself to church, but when I caught sight of her I could feel hope rising up in me. I knew she would pray for me and that there would be certainty and power in those prayers. Sometimes unexpected people may be our strongest allies in repelling unwanted predators in our lives.

Companions Who Use Space Efficiently

Using garden space efficiently is not only smart from a production standpoint but also from a health perspective. Planting the proper plants next to one another conserves space, water, and nutrients. The Three Sisters is a Native American planting method that grows corn, beans, and squash together to help each plant thrive. Corn provides a natural pole for bean vines to climb. Beans fix nitrogen on their roots, improving the overall fertility of the plot by providing nitrogen for the following year's corn. Bean vines also help stabilize the corn plants, making them less vulnerable to wind damage. Shallow-rooted squash vines become a living mulch, shading emerging weeds and preventing soil moisture from evaporating, thereby improving the crops' overall chances of survival in dry years. Spiny squash plants also help discourage predators from approaching the corn and beans. The large amount of crop residue from this planting combination can be incorporated back into the soil at the end of the season, to build up the organic matter and improve its structure.

Such companions thrive in the Body of Christ. Learning to recognize one another's gifts and calling is vital to nourishing one another with edification, hope, prayer, and unconditional love. As we grow side-by-side, it is beneficial to know next to whom you grow best. We sometimes take it as a personal insult if one person in particular does not want to be a close intimate friend to us, but that person may not be one of your two "sisters" and you both may be detrimental to one another's growth. Jesus may not have had one-on-one encounters with every person who heard him, but he still managed to touch them and change their lives forever. You might be a lettuce plant who is still in the garden in the midst of the July heat. You may not be a close personal friend with a brother or sister who is a corn plant, but their gifts shade and cool your sun-burned leaves. This has allowed you to thrive. Maybe there is a brother or sister, a green bean plant, in between the two of you, and you feel a twinge of envy because he or she lovingly holds on to the corn plant. You still can be blessed by both of them. Your sister corn is keeping you cool and your brother green bean, your friend in the row beside you, is sending nitrogen into the soil which you need lots of to make your beautiful lush leaves.

Learning to live in unity in the Body is vital to living a healthy Kingdom life. Your close companions will benefit from you and help you flourish. They will help you produce fruit in your life, and you will help them as well. Without judging or ostracizing we must learn to accept those plants in the garden who are also serving a very important role in the garden as a whole. They are feeding and encouraging many plants, while you are a companion to others. Unity does not necessarily mean close intimate relationship with everyone. It means loving everyone and allowing them to flourish where they are planted by God so that the garden's delicate ecosystem functions fully and properly.

The Body of Christ is strongest when functioning in unity under the anointing of the Holy Spirit and the divine planting of God.

"Behold, how good and how pleasant it is for brethren to dwell together in unity!"
—*Psalm 133:1 (NKJV)*

Favorite Recipe

CREAMED PEAS AND NEW POTATOES

1 1/2 cups fresh shelled peas, cooked
1 pound fresh new or baby potatoes
2 tablespoons flour
2 tablespoons butter
1 cup half-and-half
Salt and pepper to taste

Cook potatoes and peas separately until tender in lightly salted boiling water. Drain and set aside.

Cream Sauce: In medium-size pot over medium heat, melt butter and whisk in flour. Cook, whisking constantly, for 30 seconds. Do not allow this to brown. Remove from heat and slowly whisk in half-and-half. Return pot to heat and continue stirring with whisk until mixture comes to a simmer. Stir and simmer until thickened, about 1 to 2 minutes. Season with salt and pepper to taste. Remove from heat. If pot is large enough, add peas and potatoes and gently blend into sauce using a spoon. If vegetables have cooled, return pot to low heat and warm, being careful to stir constantly so cream sauce doesn't scorch. Serve hot.

Makes 4 servings.

Notes

Growing Tip

One way to amend soil and add organic matter is to sow a cover crop. Cover crops are usually legume or grain crops that add nitrogen and many other beneficial nutrients back into the soil following the harvesting of other crops. Not only do these cover crops add nutritional value to the soil but they also help to improve soil structure and volume. Beneficial cover crops include rye grasses, buckwheat, field peas, oats, and various bean crops. These are planted and allowed to grow from six inches to as much as eighteen inches. Then they are tilled or turned back into the soil. For smaller garden spaces, they are simply covered with aged wood chips or aged manure. All of this will break down, compost, and add to your soil's nutritional value and depth.

Devotion Three

The Depth of Our Roots

In Jesus' parable of the Sower, he spoke of seed that fell on various types of soil. The seed that fell by the wayside were quickly devoured by the birds. The seed that fell on stony ground sprang up quickly, but, because they had no earth to sink their roots into, withered in the heat of the sun. The seed that fell among the thorns were choked by them. And the seed that fell on good ground produced abundantly. That day, Jesus was also sowing his Word. Some of it was stolen away, some withered up, and some was choked by weeds. But some produced a great harvest and continues to do so today.

In planting seeds it is crucial that the roots have good soil in which to grow deep. The top few inches of soil is where the seed germinates and what it holds on to. The seed is nourished by it and warmed by the sun. Moisture comes into contact with the seed and begins the germination process. In the first few days after the seed is sown, the seed coat is softening and breaking open. Once germination takes place and the seed sends out its first fine roots, it is crucial that not only the top layer of soil is rich but also the soil as much as twelve inches down.

What Is Good Ground?

Good ground is rich in the nutrients necessary for basic plant nutrition, including nitrogen. It contains sufficient minerals (trace elements) for plant nutrition, including boron, chlorine, cobalt, copper, iron, manganese, magnesium, molybdenum, sulfur, and zinc. It contains soil organic matter that improves soil structure and soil moisture retention. It will have an average soil pH in the range 6.0 to 6.8 for most plants, but some plants prefer acidic or alkaline conditions. It will have good soil structure, creating well drained soil. And it will hold a range of microorganisms that support plant growth. This may seem impossible to accomplish, but God has made our soil to have much of what is needed for an abundant harvest. As we grow crops we must replenish the soil each year to assure continued health in our gardens.

Creating good ground can be accomplished by attentive soil amendment. Adding well composted organic matter to soil, rotating crops, companion planting, and allowing the soil to rest every few years will help restore the beneficial minerals, nutrients, and healthy soil structure.

Creating good ground in our lives is vital for our own fruitfulness. How can we cultivate good ground so that our lives grow and produce to the glory of God? Is there rocky ground in our lives, inhibiting growth? Are we allowing thorns or weeds to grow in our heart and soul that would choke out the seeds God's Word sows in us? How deep is our ground? Is our walk with the Lord only like seeds sown in shallow soil that stays healthy but for a brief time? Are we well rooted?

When I prepare my soil in my gardens for my vegetable crops, I work in at least four inches of well composted and aged manure. I will also add green grass clippings, dried fall leaves, and any plant residue from previous crops. By the time the process is finished I have twelve to fifteen inches of deep, rich, fertile soil. I can see the texture is good for drainage, for proper air circulation, and for roots to easily push themselves deep, enabling the plants to be well supported. When a strong summer storm comes, the plants may lean a bit and move with the gusts. After a day of sunshine, however, they are even stronger and stand taller. Their deep roots gave them the solid foundation they needed to endure the storm.

One year I was not able to be as attentive to my soil and make the additions to it that I normally do. In one short season I could see a noticeable difference not only in the soil quality but also in my crops. The plants themselves seemed tired, weak, and produced a much lower harvest.

Life can bring subtle interruptions to our intimacy with God. And they accumulate. Our prayer time is less. We haven't read our Bible in four days. We were so busy we skipped church to get the laundry done before the next week was upon us. Before we know it, our good ground is becoming fallow and our roots are starving for water and nutrition. We feel tired, weak, and the least little wind topples us. Be attentive to your good ground: Keep it rich in God's Word, listen to his voice, and pray. Praise him for his presence in your life, and seek his "good ground" for his seeds to be sown.

"Listen! Behold, a sower went out to sow. And it happened, as he sowed, that some seed fell by the wayside; and the birds of the air came and devoured it. Some fell on stony ground, where it did not have much earth; and immediately it sprang up because it had no depth of earth. But when the sun was up it was scorched, and because it had no root it withered away. And some seed fell among thorns; and the thorns grew up and choked it, and it yielded no crop. But other seed fell on good ground and yielded a crop that sprang up, increased and produced: some thirtyfold, some sixty, and some a hundred. He who has ears to hear, let him hear!"

—Matthew 13:3–9 (NKJV)

Favorite Recipe

COMPOST

Composting is fun! It brings out the mad scientist in me. In a small fenced area or purchased compost bin, add a variety of some or all of the following ingredients:

> Grass clippings
> Raw manure
> Vegetable scraps
> Dried fall leaves
> Wood shavings or straw (not hay)

Mix these together. Sprinkle a handful or two of chicken feed or high protein dog food and stir into mixture. Water well and close bin or cover pile with a tarp. Pile should heat to approximately 160°F and be stirred every week or so. If mixture seems to be dry and you do not feel heat coming from it then mix in a little more water. In a few weeks you will have compost that is rich in nutrients and organic matter—black gold. If you make your compost pile directly on the ground, you may also see lots of worms as it composts. If you compost in a bin you may still get a few worms, but not as many as compost piles that come into direct contact with the ground. When it appears all of the ingredients have broken down and you have rich, dark compost, spread on your garden.

Notes

INSPIRED GARDENING

Devotion Four

Peas in a Pod: The Joy of Growing Together

Growing Tip

Peas are a cool-weather crop. Peas thrive in cool weather and young plants will tolerate light frosts. Once germinated, peas adapt well to the cold, damp climate of early spring. Peas must be planted as early as possible in the spring to get a full harvest before hot summer temperatures arrive, putting an end to production. In temperate zones, the saying, "Plant peas by Saint Patrick's Day," holds true. Otherwise, plant peas about a month prior to your frost-free date. Always sow against a fence or provide a trellis for peas to climb on.

If you were to ask me what is the most joyful vegetable in the garden, I wouldn't hesitate before saying, "Peas." No other vegetable can make me grin and giggle the way peas growing in the garden do. For me the way they grow in community with one another makes them the epitome of joy. From vine to pod, they just love one another and they seem to love us with all their many benefits.

So before we go further, let's consider their health benefits. Peas have many phytonutrients in them. What is a phytonutrient? Phytonutrients are found in certain plants and are believed to be beneficial to human health and help prevent various diseases.

One of these phytonutrients—a polyphenol called coumestrol—has recently come to the forefront of research with respect to stomach cancer protection. Recent studies have shown that daily consumption of green peas along with other legumes lowers the risk of stomach cancer (gastric cancer), especially when daily intake from these legumes is approximately 2 mg or higher. Since one cup of green peas contains at least 10 mg of coumestrol, it's not difficult for us to obtain this remarkable health benefit.

The unique phytonutrients in green peas also provide us with key antioxidant and anti-inflammatory benefits. Included in these phytonutrients are some green pea phytonutrients called saponins. Due to their almost exclusive appearance in peas, these phytonutrients actually contain the scientific word for peas, *Pisum*, in their names: pisumsaponins I and II, and pisomosides A and B. When coupled with other phytonutrients in green peas—including phenolic acids such as ferulic and caffeic acid, and flavanols like catechin and epicatechin—the combined impact on our health may be far-reaching. For example, some researchers have now speculated that the association between green pea and legume intake and lowered risk of type 2 diabetes may be connected not only with the relatively low glycemic index of green peas (about 45–50) and their strong fiber and protein content, but also with this unusual combination of antioxidant and anti-inflammatory phytonutrients.

Peas are also an incredible asset to the health of garden soil. Agricultural research has shown that pea crops can provide the soil with important benefits. First, peas belong to a category of crops that are nitrogen-fixing. With the help of bacteria in the soil, peas are able to take nitrogen from the air and convert it into more complex and usable forms. This process increases the nitrogen available in the soil without the need for added fertilizer. Second, peas also have a relatively shallow root system which can help prevent erosion of the soil. And once the peas have been picked, the plant remainders tend to break down relatively easily for soil replenishment. Finally, the rotation of peas with other crops has been shown to lower the risk of pest problems. These environmentally friendly aspects of pea production add to their desirability as a regular part of our diet and our garden plan.

My favorite variety of pea to grow is the English pea. This is the shelling variety that most of your canned and frozen peas in the store come from. There are of course other varieties, such as sugar snap peas and the snow peas, which can be eaten pod and all. Though some vine less than others, all varieties of peas vine to some extent. English peas are the variety that vine the tallest.

One of the characteristics of peas that make them seem so joyful to me is their tendrils. As the plant grows, the main stem grows up and sends out other stems that have thread-fine tendrils on them. The tendrils reach out and grab hold of the closest stabilizing force, such as a trellis or a fence. And the best thing about their tendrils is that they will even grab hold of one another. It is wonderful to see. These beautiful, curly green tendrils reach out and hold on to the pea vine growing next to them. When an entire row of pea plants is growing next to one another, they seem to be embracing, holding on to each other lovingly.

Then there are the flowers. Beautiful in shape, color, and appearance, they seem to be smiling, happy to be a part of this pea family. Even as the flowers make their exit, they don't dry up and turn an ugly brown like some vegetables' flowers do, but they just sort of gracefully fall to the ground, still lovely and white. The flower humbly bows out to make way for a tiny flat pod that forms right behind the flower on the same stem. As the pod grows, the peas inside are forming and filling out. Soon the pod is chubby and full and ready to be harvested. They make the perfect garden snack. Many a day while weeding or sowing new seeds, I will walk to my row of pea plants and pick a few pods. They even make it handy and easy to snack on them fresh, by just popping them open from their built-in zipper seam down the edge of the pod. Their sweet goodness can be savored immediately.

As I pick my first English peas of the season each spring, I can't help but admire them inside their pods. Snuggled together tightly and each pea perfectly shaped and sized, no one pea seems to want to outdo another. They grow equal in size, sharing space and nutrients lovingly. They actually look so content and happy to be together that I hate to pop them out. But they are so fresh and sweet and irresistible—a blessing indeed.

As I see these snuggling peas, I can't help but wonder whether I could be so close to and generous with others. God places people in our lives whom we can bless and serve. We can learn godly characteristics by watching the peas: We should reach out to others with our tendrils and support each other while we grow. This habit establishes unity and strength within the body of believers. We ought to rejoice and smile as we bloom as well as humbly and gracefully stepping aside so that others can flourish and begin the process of producing fruit. As we live and grow with others, we gladly share space and nutrition, and ultimately celebrate together as our fruit creates a harvest. Growing together brings strength. Mutual support lends itself to bearing fruit together, which blesses God as we become a family that is one.

"Be kindly affectionate to one another with brotherly love, in honor giving preference to one another."

—*Romans 12:10 (NKJV)*

Favorite Recipe

PEAS AND MUSHROOMS

2 cups shelled fresh peas
1 package (8-ounce) sliced mushrooms
2 tablespoons butter
Salt and pepper to taste

Shell and rinse peas in cold water. Bring pot of salted water to boil. Add peas and cook until tender, about 2 to 3 minutes, or until crisp and tender, but not mushy. Drain peas and set aside. In sauté pan melt butter and add mushrooms. Season lightly with salt and pepper. Sauté mushrooms until liquid is evaporated and they just start to brown lightly. Remove pan from heat and toss peas into sauté pan. Mix together and place in serving dish.

Makes 4 servings.

Notes

Growing Tip

In late August or early September—or anytime in winter with a plastic hoop cover over a small raised bed—prepare a bed of loose soil rich in composted organic matter, such as aged manure, turned lightly into soil. Sow spinach seed right on top of soil. Then lightly brush your hand over the soil, working the seed into the soil, about ¼-inch deep. Keep moist until germination. As temperatures get colder, and especially at night, cover bed with fall leaves to about 1 to 2 inches deep. Add more leaves as the months pass, and when winter's snows come just let the snow cover the leaves. The leaves will insulate the spinach plants and they will continue growing, though a bit slower. But they will thrive and live comfortably under their blanket of snow and leaves. When you crave a spinach salad in the midst of winter's cold, simply brush back the snow and leaves and harvest fresh spinach.

Devotion Five

Growing in the Winter of Our Life

Are we living in the season we are in? My garden teaches me so much about my heavenly Father, his heart, and his thoughts toward us. And, importantly, it has taught me to live in the season I am in. I have learned that when it is winter, even in rest, there is growth. I have a tendency to sometimes strive with God. I always want something to be happening. I have to do this; I have to do that. And I impatiently wonder, "Why aren't things moving faster?" I am beginning to understand that sometimes it is winter. It's OK for me to rest and rejuvenate. It's OK that I can't do, do, do in this season. Especially when the means to act are out of my reach or control. Plant life in winter is all but nonexistent (a few plants are exceptions, whose purpose it is to grow in winter and actually produce a harvest). But just because we cannot see leaves and fruit does not mean there isn't anything going on beneath the soil.

Wintertime is a blessing for soil. It is the time when soil is rebuilding by resting. While it appears as if all activity in the garden has stopped, there's a lot going on under the soil until it freezes. Newly transplanted trees and shrubs, divisions of perennials, and hardy bulbs are all growing roots, drawing on soil nutrients and moisture around them. Earthworms and various microbes in the soil are still processing the organic material they're finding. Most likely, the organic mulch you spread to protect the soil during the summer months has substantially decomposed. It's important to spread new mulch now—a thicker winter layer—to protect plants and soil over the winter months. The idea is not so much to keep the soil warm as it is to keep the temperature even. Once the soil is frozen, mulch keeps it frozen. So if you have shade trees, convert the fallen leaves to mulch and use it throughout your garden.

Snow can seem so cold and harsh. But did you know that snow itself can act as a mulch, protecting the plants? In fact, farmers in the old days used to refer to snow as the "poor man's fertilizer." Snow, as it is falling, captures atmospheric nitrogen. As the snow melts, it slowly releases the nitrogen into the soil. In spring, new emerging seedlings will take advantage of this nitrogen source as the soil thaws and water starts traveling through the soil.

As we put our gardens to sleep for winter, frozen and covered with mulch, we too can feel as cold and barren as the beds look when we peer out the window toward them, longing for warmer, green-filled days. During these insulated days, rather than allow loneliness or isolation to surround us, we can draw deeper and closer to the heart of God. God is never asleep, never frozen, never barren. He is always restoring all things so that we are prepared for the next season of growth. Rest is vital, restoration and rejuvenation brings back hope and inspiration—our vision for the next season.

One of my favorite leafy green vegetables to grow is spinach. I have grown spinach in spring and, though it produces a harvest,

I have noticed spinach does not do as well in the warmer days of late spring or early summer. It seems less vibrant, to have less flavor and yield a smaller harvest.

One year I decided to sow some spinach seeds in very early fall. I planted in September and, with the lingering warm days of fall, the seeds had plenty of time to germinate and get a good strong start as seedlings. Knowing that spinach is a hardy leafy green plant that can withstand cooler temps, I mulched the plants with fall leaves in October, hoping the plants would continue to grow as the colder nights set in with potential frosts. The plants thrived even in the colder weather, and I was able to harvest fresh spinach leaves right through November. Then one night in December, we got six inches of snow. The temperature stayed below freezing, and so the snow lingered for quite a few days. As I walked around the beds, I took in the emptiness of the snow-covered gardens. They looked so cold and lonely, similar to how I was feeling that day. I approached the bed where the spinach had been growing. I noticed the dry fall leaves poking out from beneath the snow layer. As I crouched down to give a fond touch to the bed, my hand nudged aside one of the brown brittle leaves. To my surprise, I caught a glimpse of deep green color. As I brushed away the layer of snow and pulled off some of the fall leaves, I discovered a huge, healthy, vibrant-green spinach plant. This plant had new baby leaves emerging from the center of it and large leaves ready for harvest in a beautiful outer circle. I stared at this lush green plant, for what seemed like a very long time, in amazement. Here was this beautiful plant thriving and loving its environment in spite of the harsh cold of its surroundings. I knew that the deep green color was probably being accomplished by the slow release of nitrogen coming from the thaw of the snow in the sunshine each day: leafy greens love nitrogen. As I harvested enough spinach for a lovely salad, my heart was full of thanks to God for revealing to me the truth that no matter our circumstances, we can thrive and grow and produce glorious fruit with his love and protection—and a little mulch and snow. Even in the freezing seasons of our life, there is growth. We will not utterly die if we stay insulated by God's Word and rest in his love and the safety of his will for our lives.

"The rain and snow come down from the heavens and stay on the ground to water the earth. They cause the grain to grow, producing seed for the farmer and bread for the hungry."
—*Isaiah 55:10 (NKJV)*

Garden Recipe

SPINACH AND PEAR SALAD

This is a lovely salad blend of fresh-from-your-garden spinach and the sweet pears of fall.

8 cups lightly packed fresh baby spinach leaves, stemmed if needed

2 firm but ripe Bosc pears (do not peel), quartered lengthwise, cored, and cut into long, thin slices

1 cup thinly sliced red onion

1/3 cup sweetened dried cranberries

2/3 cup hazelnuts, toasted and chopped

In large bowl mix all salad ingredients and toss lightly. Transfer salad blend into serving bowl and serve with a dressing made of 2 parts olive oil to 1 part balsamic vinegar.

Notes

Devotion Six

Do You Need to Be Fertilized?

Growing Tip

When fertilizing your garden, be sure to use the proper fertilizer for each crop you are growing. Using a general fertilizer is not always the best choice. Leafy green vegetables need a fertilizer high in nitrogen, root crops prefer phosphorus, and so on. So research your particular veggie first, then feed it.

I got a call from a friend who shared that she felt, "discouraged, tired, weary, and just plain yuk!" The day she called I had been out in the garden fertilizing, because some of my veggie plants looked exactly how my friend felt. They were pale green, some leaves were yellowing, they had spindly growth, and they just looked tired. So I said to my friend, "Sounds like you need some 10-10-10." Since she is also a gardener, she immediately understood what I meant.

10-10-10 is a general all-purpose fertilizer for vegetables. The scientific formula is NPK: nitrogen, phosphorus, and potassium.

So here is a brief lesson on what 10-10-10 stands for and does in your garden:
- Nitrogen: The first number of an NPK rating grows big plants with lots of leaves.

- Phosphorus: The middle number is best known as the nutrient that produces more flowers and fruits, but it's also essential to strong root growth early in the season.
- Potassium: The third number helps plants process all nutrients more efficiently, improves the quality of fruits, and helps plants resist stress.

When I felt God giving me this particular devotional, I thought (or maybe I said to him), "That's silly! How can I turn fertilizer into a spiritual lesson?" As soon as I said it, God told me to go out to the garden. I receive most of my spiritual insight in the garden, especially when I am being a contrary child. Isn't it wonderful how much our Daddy God loves us? So off I trotted to my garden.

As I sat and looked at my plants (yes, I sit in my garden), my Father spoke to me, saying, "What makes the plants lush and green and vibrant?"

"Nitrogen," I said.

"When they are lush and vibrant they look happy, right?"

"Well, yes, they do, as a matter of fact."

"How do you feel and how do you look when you spend time in my presence and we talk and love on one another?" he said.

"I feel happy, content, energized, and healthy."

"So nitrogen is the same to plants as spending time in my presence is for you."

Aha! I got it! So I felt God smile on me, and he got quiet so I could figure out the rest. See, that is how we reflect more of his image, when we become like-minded with Christ and our Father.

Phosphorus in our walk is the Word of God and prayer. We need strong roots and depth of understanding in our life with Christ. Spending time in the Bible and getting to know the heart of God through his true Word is the way to develop strong roots, so that when the storms come we cannot be knocked over and blown about. As our roots grow deeper and we become stronger, we will produce more fruit in our life and start blessing others with that same fruit.

Potassium in our Christian life is the Body of Christ—fellowshipping and worshipping with the brethren. (Don't you love the word, *brethren*? I do.) The fellowship with the brethren helps us process our nutrients (teachings and ministry) better. They help improve the quality of our fruit by encouraging and edifying us to use our fruit for the benefit of others, rather than keep it all to ourselves. And the brethren help us relieve stress by being our friends, prayer warriors, and comrades in arms!

So are you taking in enough fertilizer? Are you spending intimate, passionate, private time with your Father and your Savior? Are you studying, reading, and digesting God's Word? And are you a member of a family of believers whom you consider your brethren? If you are doing only one or two of these things, then you will lack certain nutrients that will make you a complete plant in God's garden. You may topple over easily due to shallow, weak roots. Or you may be yellow and tired and unable to testify of God's goodness because of your sad countenance. You may be an easy target for the enemy, because you are alone and not part of a family of believers who will cover you in prayer in times of need. Just as plants need a balanced growing environment to fulfill their purpose and produce a harvest; so we also need to walk with the Lord, spending time with him and with his Word, and to be faithful and encouraging to one another in order to to be complete and healthy, and to fully grow. Ask God what you may be lacking, and then get yourself fertilized. Remember that for optimum growing conditions, a balanced fertilizer is best.

"Beloved, I pray that you may prosper in all things and be in health, just as your soul prospers."
—3 John 1:2 (NKJV)

Notes

Devotion Seven

Finding Our Place

Growing Tip

Artichoke plants can be very big, so spacing is vital. Plant three to five feet apart. Yes, feet. The plants can get very big. They also can handle part sun in warmer zones. Artichokes can be grown as perennials in Zone 7 or higher but are grown as annuals in the cooler zones.

All plants have specific requirements in order to thrive and reach their potential. How much sunlight plants receive is one of those requirements. There are plants that require full sun, part sun, and shade. Full sun is defined by a minimum of six to eight hours of full sun, Part sun is defined by a minimum of four to six hours of sun. Shade is defined as mottled sun or protected growing from full sun.

For the past two growing seasons I have attempted to grow artichokes. I love artichokes. They are a favorite of many Italian families like mine. During my childhood my mother made these delicacies only once a year because they were very time-consuming to prepare. Just thinking about them has my mouth watering. However, the price of artichokes has risen substantially since my childhood. Not being one to shy away from a challenge, I decided to research the growing zones and requirements of this beautiful vegetable that is actually a flower bud.

In the first year of my planting trials, the seedlings grew about two inches and then slowly died. In the second year, I planted new seedlings in a different location of my garden trying to achieve the perfect conditions; these seedlings lasted a few weeks and grew a bit bigger, but eventually they also died. No matter how much tender loving care I gave them in the form of organic matter, fertilizer, and water; they never seemed to be happy or at rest just growing. They always struggled. I thought that perhaps they couldn't grow well in my zone and needed very controlled growing conditions; so I would just have to throw in the gardening gloves and resort to buying artichokes once every five years to satisfy my cravings. At least for a season. A faithful gardener never really gives up unless we're talking oranges or lemons — then we just need to be realistic. (Unless you are in Zone 9 or higher, of course.)

Eventually I decided to do a bit more research in the form of posting questions on some of my favorite gardening groups online. Sure enough, within a couple of days, I got some replies from people in my zone who had grown artichokes successfully. I learned a few more tips and ventured out to try one more time. I got more seedlings and went out to my garden. I set the babies on the ground and prayed a quick prayer. Not really hearing a "Thus saith the Lord" about what to do, I picked up the seedlings and planted in a new area that was suitable for all the light and space requirements I had read about. I made a cozy corner bed against the garden fence about two to three feet wide and about ten inches deep. I made a mix of rich soil, compost and manure and a little fertilizer for good measure. I talked to the seedlings as I planted them, prayed over them, and, in faith, got out of the way.

Finding the right place is so important. Knowing who you are, what God has planned for you, your destiny and purpose in the Kingdom, and who you are in his eyes. We surely will struggle and eventually die emotionally and spiritually if we strive to grow and fulfill a proscribed purpose in a place outside of God's will. The church in which you belong, the job, the marriage, and even the friendships, all need to be orchestrated and led by the Holy Spirit according to his will for your life and no one else's.

You cannot be a cucumber if you are destined to be an artichoke. Being planted in the perfect place can be the difference between a destiny fulfilled or a life of turmoil and frustration. Obedience, trust, faith, and surrender to the Father are the way to ensure you are in the perfect place for you. You are the only one who can serve the purpose and calling God designed for you; you are unique and special, and he needs you.

That third planting of artichoke seedlings? Well they took off and are doing beautifully. They are content, happy, healthy, and on their way to blessing us with a harvest of beautiful and delicious artichokes.

Favorite Recipe

OK, so I don't have a favorite artichoke recipe, because I have only stuffed them—each individual leaf (Yes, it is tedious)—with a seasoned bread crumb, parmesan cheese, and olive oil mixture. Lay the artichoke on its side and make a slice across the top of the artichoke cutting off all the pointy leaf tips. Left whole, the individual leaves are gently opened and stuffed with a seasoned bread crumb mixture, and then each whole artichoke is gently placed in a deep pot that has enough water in the bottom to just touch the bottom of the artichokes. They are tightly placed in the pan so that they remain upright, and then steamed until the leaves come away easily from the stem when gently pulled. The bottom half of the leaf and stuffing is eaten.

STUFFING MIX

2 cups seasoned bread crumbs
1/2 cup grated parmesan cheese
About 1/8 cup olive oil

Mix together. Add more oil if mixture is still dry and doesn't hold together loosely.

Notes

Notes

INSPIRED GARDENING

Devotion Eight

Some Things Just Take Time

Growing Tip

When planting new asparagus crowns be sure you start with a 12-inch-deep bed of loose, well-draining soil. Lots of compost and organic matter, such as aged manure, is perfect for the crowns and a handful of bone meal around each crown before covering will give them a good start to life.

One day about three years after I started growing vegetables, I was in the supermarket strolling through the produce section. I came upon what is possibly my favorite vegetable, asparagus. The sign read, "$3.99 lb." I looked at the sign, looked at the asparagus, and thought, "Are they kidding?" I walked on disappointed and with a craving for asparagus. Suddenly, I thought to myself, "I wonder if asparagus will grow in North Carolina?" I always thought asparagus would only grow in California. I am not really sure where I got that notion, but I thought it must be so.

As soon as I got home I went online and started my research. Sure enough asparagus did grow in my zone! How exciting! I found a grower of asparagus plants, and ordered twenty-five of them. I always start big. While I was doing my research though, I learned that asparagus is grown from crowns. Crowns are roots with a crown-looking center (hence the name) that the spears emerge from. The asparagus is one of the first veggies of spring and produce for about eight weeks. The chink in the armor of my asparagus craving is that the crowns do not produce spears big enough to harvest until they are three years old. The advantage to asparagus crowns is that they produce for more than ten years; asparagus is a perennial vegetable. So once planted it is best to leave it in a permanent bed and allow it to grow there long term. I found a grower online that sold two-year-old crowns, which cuts off one year of waiting. I was so excited to be able to grow my own asparagus that I couldn't hardly stand the anticipation of the first harvest.

Now there are many aspects of growing your own food that holds people back from gardening. But for me, in all my years of gardening, for me the wait is the hardest. I mean let's look at this. You plant in my zone starting sometime in February, getting the soil ready and cleaning up from last year if you didn't do it in the fall. Then in March you start sowing the cool weather veggie seeds. Then you work on the rest of the garden to get ready for planting the warm weather crops. By May you are finally planting tomatoes, squash, cucumbers, etc. And weeding the spring veggies but still waiting on some yumminess. Finally, by June or early July, you are harvesting the things you planted back in March and April and are waiting for that first red tomato. And if you planted winter squash, then don't hold your breath: You ain't tasting those till September or October! Gardening is a waiting game.

Which brings us back to asparagus. When I ordered my first crowns, I learned that asparagus grows male or female. You do not need both male and female plants to get asparagus, and so male crowns are preferred by growers because they produce more vegetables. Although the female crowns do produce spears, they also put a lot of energy into making seeds. For this reason, most growers sell only male crowns. In my first order of crowns, however, I happened to get one female crown. So when my crowns were three years old, I got an abundance of seeds from this little gal in my garden. I decided to try my hand at germinating these seeds, with success. They germinated well. So after the first year in the greenhouse, I planted them out in their own raised bed in the garden. Though they had already spent an entire year in my greenhouse, now they were going to have to sit in the bed for another two years before we could harvest asparagus from them. Talk about a waiting game. I could see the crowns getting bigger by the way they were sending up these skinny little spears. They were dark green and vigorous and apparently happy. But when would the spears be big enough to harvest? The wait seemed to last forever.

Are you waiting for a harvest from a prayer you planted long ago? We plant our prayers in God's garden. Some prayers, like some veggies, produce quick. That is, God quickly gives a harvest, and it is full and complete. But other prayers take longer to produce. Even though we planted them with faith, it is hard to walk by that area of our garden knowing we planted that prayer but not yet seeing the harvest. But as time and the seasons pass, there is growth that we just do not see. There are things happening under the soil. The roots are getting stronger and going deeper. In its perfect time, God will provide the harvest. Not early, not late. The fruit will be produced and its purpose will be fulfilled. But we must leave the plant (prayer) undisturbed. We must not become impatient and take the plant back, digging it up saying, "Well, maybe if I move it to this part of the garden it will grow faster." In doing so we have disturbed the roots and possibly injured what has already been accomplished.

I had a friend who was an experienced gardener. He would teach me about growing vegetables, and one of his biggest pet peeves was when people fussed too much with their gardens and plants. One of my favorite sayings he had was, "Make a nice soil bed, plant the seed, give them a little fertilizer, and get out of the way!"

That is what we must do with our prayers. Pray to the Father, make known our requests, place it in his hands, and get out of the way! Allow God to be God. He is the creator, he has the answers, and he will make the prayer produce the harvest.

> *"Again he prayed, and the heavens gave rain, and the earth produced its crops."*
> *—James 5:18 (NKJV)*

Favorite Recipe

ROASTED ASPARAGUS

1 pound fresh asparagus
Olive oil
Salt and pepper to taste

Snap the tough ends off of each spear. Rinse under cold water and pat dry. In a single layer, lay spears out on a broiler pan. Brush lightly with olive oil and season with salt and pepper. Roast 5 to 7 minutes until spears are crisp and tender. Serve immediately. (These can be prepared the same way on a grill.)

Notes

Devotion Nine

God Wants to Compost You

Growing Tip

When making a compost pile, create an area that is away from your house and close to your garden area. This makes less work when bringing your compost to the garden. Make a simple fenced circle or square out of metal T-posts and rigid wire fencing in order to contain the pile and make turning the compost easier. Old sturdy pallets are also good for making a three-sided boxed area for your pile. Simply layer your materials, water, and mix occasionally. Be sure to add small twigs between the layers to create air pockets. Do not pack the layers tightly: You want air and water to be able to circulate.

Compost is a wonderful thing. It is rich in nutrients, and, when added to dirt in your garden, it makes a fertile humus that plants will thrive in. Most gardeners like to add their grass clippings from mowing their lawns to their compost piles. Weeds from the garden are also great to compost. But grass clippings and weeds that are pulled from your garden can have seeds in them, which, when the compost is added to the soil, will just create more weeds. In order to kill the weed seeds, the compost pile needs to reach 140°F and stay at that temperature for one to three days, depending on the kind of weeds.

I have also added horse manure to my garden, which in itself is wonderful for the soil and the plants. But the way a horse digests the hay and grains it eats leads to unprocessed seeds in its manure. When added to your soil, you can end up with a lovely bed of hay when you intended on growing roses. So the manure must be composted properly. You do not want to compost the manure so long that all the nutritional benefits in it are depleted, but long enough and hot enough to kill the hay and grain seeds. Composting is a science, literally. A compost pile must have the proper ratio of ingredients to break down and make compost. A good ratio is approximately 30:1, 30 parts carbon (brown material) to 1 part nitrogen (green material). Good ingredients for carbon include dried leaves, straw, peanut shells, shredded cardboard, and wood chips. Good nitrogen ingredients include grass clippings, plant residue, weeds, food waste (never oils, fats, or meats), coffee grounds, vegetable scraps, and fresh manures.

Layering is the best method of composting—alternate layers of brown and green materials and water with air pockets. *Brown* and *green* refers to dried leaves, small twigs, straw, aged manure for brown. Plant residue, grass clippings, kitchen vegetable scraps for green. The breakdown of the materials is what creates the heat. Turning the pile occasionally helps mix the ingredients and create necessary air passages. After a nice cooking period, you will see the ingredients in your pile turning into organic matter and smelling like earth rather than grass clippings. This is when it is ready to add to your garden. Properly composted materials will be a nutritious boost to your soil and plants and will give you a healthier garden.

Have you ever felt like sometimes you are being suffocated by weeds? Or that there are so many weeds seeds sprouting up around you that you can't pull them out fast enough? Life has weeds. Some are small and easy to pull out like clover, and seem to pop up frequently. Then there are the tough invasive weeds like crabgrass. Their roots go deep and they spread quickly. When you do pull it out, you are never quite sure if you got it all. The small weeds are daily annoyances, such as rude people or forgetting to lock the door. If we let them, these little annoyances will steal our peace from us, creating frustration and stress. They will draw us away from godly mindsets, and soon we will be functioning out of a place of impatience and anger. Crabgrass is like a character trait or bad habit that we know is not pleasing to God, but we are not sure whether it is a sin. So we end up justifying it or trying to live with it, since we don't think it's hurting anyone. Eventually it spreads throughout your life, choking the word planted in your life and making you unfruitful.

God watches our life: he listens to all our prayers; he journaled about all our days.

> *"Your eyes saw my unformed body;*
> *all the days ordained for me were written in your book*
> *before one of them came to be."*
> *—Psalm 139:16, NKJV*

He sees things that we don't see as well as the things we do see and try to hide. He sees when we try to live with a bad habit like an annoying weed in the garden. Sometimes even pulling a weed out by its root does not clear the garden of it for good. We must toss the weed and all its roots and seeds into the compost pile to kill it completely. Not until then will we have clean, healthy soil. What weeds do you see in your life that you are willing to pull out and toss in the compost pile for God to turn into organic matter? Get alone in a quiet, secret place with God. Tune out any distractions. Close your eyes, and ask God to show you what weeds are in your life. As he does, envision yourself ripping them up and taking them to the compost pile. Mix them in so they get up to temperature, and kill the root and the seeds that may keep the weed resprouting over and over again in your life. We can have a hurt, an ungodly habit, or a character flaw that lies dormant for a season. When the conditions are just right, however, that weed sprouts with a vengeance, and spreads, taking over the healthy growth in our life. Even when we think we have pulled up the weed, there may be hidden seeds, or triggers, that cause it to sprout. God can clean those seeds and the root out of our life completely so that we can grow strong and healthy, producing much fruit for his glory.

Getting our own compost pile hot enough to kill the seeds may be uncomfortable, but it is necessary to be sure the seeds are dead and will not sprout again. God will walk us through periods like this that makes it seem as if we are in the fire and it seems unbearable. But he will never leave us in so long that we are destroyed. He will only leave us in the fire long enough to purify and cleanse us of the weed's seeds, in order to change us into a rich, nutrient-filled organic matter that is fertile and productive. When we are sent back to the garden and become part of the soil, we enrich it and produce an abundant harvest. Isn't it like our God to take annoying, potentially fruit-destroying weeds, and transforming them into a beneficial, life-giving material?

I want to be composted. I want to be as rich and productive and healthy as God created me to be. The world is a garden, and we are the compost that enriches it.

"And we all, who with unveiled faces contemplate the Lord's glory, are being transformed into his image with ever-increasing glory, which comes from the Lord, who is the Spirit."
—*2 Corinthians 3:18 (NKJV)*

Notes

Notes

INSPIRED GARDENING

Devotion Ten

Be What You Were Created to Be

Growing Tip

Journal your garden each year. Draw a diagram of the garden layout, then label your rows within the drawing. Because I grow three different plantings—early spring, summer, and early fall—I make three different drawings. I not only label the sections or rows to remind me where things are planted but I also write down the dates when they are sown, germinate, harvested, and how much they produced. I make notes about the particular veggie variety to remind me that I liked it or didn't particularly cared for it. This sounds like a lot of detail. But it only takes a few moments, and it is worth it year-to-year so that you can learn from what you have done and plant a more productive garden.

After growing vegetables for about four years, my garden had grown to be nearly a full acre. Keeping track of what is planted and where it is planted is vital with a garden this size. One day I went out to plant some more seeds, and, since I am a big advocate of companion planting, I wanted to be sure to plant one vegetable next to another that would be beneficial to the one I was planting. I was really busy that year and had grown complacent about faithfully journaling my sowing. I always recommend keeping a yearly garden journal.

I stood in my garden with seeds in hand next to a row that I had planted a few days earlier. For the life of me, I could not remember what I planted. I was pretty sure it was cucumbers, so felt confident I could plant the beet seeds I held in my hand in this area since they are friendly neighbors in the garden. About the only veggie cucumbers do not like to be planted near are potatoes. So I sowed my beets and went about the rest of my day.

A few days later, as I was walking out to my garden, I spotted my cucumber seedlings emerging. I smiled because this sight is always such a wonder to me. But as I drew closer, I stopped in my tracks and saw that they were beans. I said out loud, "You're not cucumbers!" Uh-oh! I thought I was planting beets next to my cucumbers. Fortunately, beets like beans too. Phew! It made me smile again thinking that I could stand there and tell those beans they have to be cucumbers all day long, but that wouldn't change them into cucumbers. They wouldn't reply, "OK, we will make cucumbers on our bean plants."

When we sow a bean seed, we can be sure we are going to get beans. Seeds become what they were created to become. A bean plant can't say, "Look at that beautiful vining cucumber plant. So tall and wispy with beautiful yellow flowers and delicious cucumbers. I want to be like that!" Try as it might, and resist as it may, that bean plant will not, and cannot become a cucumber plant.

We all were created to become what the Father placed in us when he formed us. We may struggle for years with that destiny, because to us it doesn't look as perfect as another person's destiny. You may have been created to be an intercessor, but you envy the worship leader and want to lead worship. You may have been created to sing and may have been given an amazing singing gift. But because of your shyness, you do not want to be in front of people singing; you want to have a behind-the-scenes calling.

Some of us will strive with God for years, running after a call that is not from God. We beat down doors that were not meant to be opened; or worse, we rebel and dig our heels in saying, "No," to God when he speaks to our hearts of our true calling and destiny. Sometimes we are just afraid because of our insecurities, and so we hide behind an identity that feels safe.

Seeking God and his plan for us is the most fruitful thing we can do in our relationship with him. Once we are confident and at peace about what we know our destiny to be, we can sow our seeds with confidence and faith. Contentment will surely overtake us as we accept with joy that we are meant to be a bean. We will be able to look at our neighbor without envy, admiring their beauty and calling, and even complimenting or blessing their fulfillment. We cannot change what God has created.

"For the gifts and the calling of God are irrevocable."
—*Romans 11:29 (NKJV)*

Notes

INSPIRED GARDENING

Devotion Eleven

Patience and Winter Squash

Growing Tip

Sow winter squash varieties according to growing days on seed packets. Plant in area where vines can spread out. When squash forms, place a plate or flat stone under the squash so that it is up off the ground while growing. This helps prevent borers from getting into the squash and it also prevents rot. Fertilize after plants have established with a balanced fertilizer, such as organic vegetable fertilizer. When flowers form, feed once more according to fertilizer directions.

Whoever said "Patience is a virtue" must have grown winter squash at one time or another. Winter squash could easily be considered the most valuable and productive vegetable a gardener can grow. Most varieties produce abundant crops of delicious and very nutritious squash that is as productive in the kitchen as it is in the garden. Winter squash is a favorite at our house. I use it as a side dish, in dessert pies, in a wonderful bisque, in a delicious tea bread or cake, and I have even used it to make a yeast-dough, braided coffee cake.

But growing winter squash takes patience. Where summer and zucchini squash can seemingly grow from finger-size to baseball-bat-size overnight, some varieties of winter squash can take as many as 120 days to produce. The shortest variety I have personally grown is about an 80-day acorn squash.

In an earlier devotion, I shared my favorite winter

squash, Musquee de Provence. This variety will provide a huge amount of squash, but it easily takes 100 to 120 days from sowing to harvest. Equally tasty is the butternut squash. Though each squash is not as large as a Musquee pumpkin, butternut is easy to grow, reliable, and produces, on average, four to six squash per plant. Butternut squash can take 100 days to mature.

Planting according to your zone is key when growing winter squash because even though *winter* is in their name, they are not cold-hardy plants. Temperatures much below 40°F will damage the plants, and a frost will surely kill them off, so it is important to know the number of growing days for your zone and count backward from four weeks before your average first frost. For example, in my zone my average first-frost date is October 30, so I am always sure to have my winter squash planted by June 20. As you can see winter squash takes forethought, planning, and patience. But it is so worth it!

Many times we sow seeds in faith hoping for a harvest. But the wait seems to go on forever. God promises that through our faith and waiting on him he will answer our prayers and we will receive that which he has promised us. "We do not want you to become lazy, but to imitate those who through faith and patience inherit what has been promised" (Hebrews 6:12, NIV). It is difficult at times to wait for the seed to produce a harvest, and sometimes the seeds fail. But do we give up and lose heart? No, we sow again and believe that God will bring forth a harvest.

What do we do while we wait?

Patience does not mean waiting with anxiety. Vine's Expository Dictionary defines patience as "an abiding under." Rest and abide in his presence, and find peace in the moment. Moreover, patience is not sitting and doing nothing. After we sow the squash seeds, we don't just sit down and stare at the place we planted the seed. We go about the other needs of the garden: tending other plants that are close to harvest, pulling weeds, fertilizing. I find while I am practicing patience—because patience does not come easy for me — I must practice it by taking on other responsibilities. Keeping occupied with other tasks helps. I prepare the soil, sow the squash seeds, say a prayer over the sowing, and then I leave the rest to God and get out of his way.

When my son was three years old, I planted some marigold seeds with him in front of our house. Each day he would go out and push the dirt away from the spot we planted, looking for the flowers. Over and over I tried to explain to him that you must leave the seeds alone and let them do what God made them to do. Then they would grow and make the flowers. He just couldn't wait. After a few days of a three-year-old searching for flowers, I knew the seeds had been too disturbed to germinate. So I went to the garden center, bought a marigold plant, hid it until he went to bed, and then I planted it. When he woke up the next day, sure enough, he asked if he could go out and look for his flowers. We got dressed, and off he ran out the door to discover this big, beautiful, flowering plant. The joy and amazement on his face was incredible. It seemed to him that he had endured patiently, but in reality he had messed with the seed so much that it never produced a harvest. As a mom, I wanted to bless my son with seeing the fruit of his sowing. Many times we adults fuss with our prayer seeds too much. We pray and walk away. But then the next morning when we don't yet see any fruit, we start digging around and wondering why God isn't doing anything. We take the seed back, get in God's way, and can actually delay the harvest or hinder it all together.

Patience is a virtue to be practiced and mastered. So if you struggle with waiting on God to answer prayer seeds you have planted, sow some winter squash in June. In November when you are savoring the rich sweetness of that deep orange goodness, think back to June and how you thought this day would never come. The harvest will be abundant, and your patience will be rewarded.

> "But those who wait on the Lord shall renew their strength; they shall mount up with wings like eagles, they shall run and not be weary, they shall walk and not faint."
>
> —*Isaiah 40:31 (NKJV)*

Favorite Recipe

WINTER SQUASH ROLLS

3 1/2 cups all-purpose flour
1 package (.25 ounce) active dry yeast
2 eggs
1/2 cup winter squash puree
1/2 cup warm water (110ºF)
4 tablespoons white sugar
3 tablespoons butter, softened
1 teaspoon salt

Dissolve yeast, warm water, and 1 tablespoon sugar in a mixing bowl. Let stand 5 minutes.

Add remaining sugar, squash, butter, salt, and slightly beaten eggs. Stir to mix well. Stir in 3 cups of flour. Turn out on a lightly floured surface. Knead 2 to 3 minutes, adding just enough of remaining flour to prevent sticking. Do not knead too heavily; when smooth, shape into a ball. Place in an oiled bowl, and turn to coat the surface. Cover, and let rise about 1 hour or longer.

Punch down, and allow dough to rest for 2 minutes. Divide into 16 to 20 balls, and place on a greased cookie sheet or in a 9 x 13–inch pan. Allow to rise until doubled. Bake at 375ºF for 12 to 20 minutes.

Serve warm.

Bread Machine: Add ingredients to bread machine according to instructions. Set machine to Dough Cycle. Remove dough and continue with shaping, allow second rise, and bake.

Notes

Devotion Twelve

Indeterminate Blessings

Growing Tip

When vegetables are abundantly producing and the growing season is winding down, they sometimes don't look their best, and some are even inedible. These are the ones I save seeds from. Cut the fruit of the plant open, removing the seeds. Spread them out on a paper-towel-lined cookie sheet and allow them to air-dry in a warm place with good air circulation. I lay mine on my kitchen table with the ceiling fan on low. Gently move the seeds around every few days. When the seeds feel completely dry, seal them in an airtight container, label, and date. This process will give you your own organic heirloom seeds for next year's garden and some to share with other gardeners.

In the Bible God calls us to be generous, and he promises to bless us when we are. God's Word has a lot to say about the connection between generous giving and blessings: "A generous person will prosper; whoever refreshes others will be refreshed" (Proverbs 11:25, NIV), or "The generous will themselves be blessed, for they share their food with the poor" (Proverbs 22:9, NIV).

Even the poorest among us are called to live generously. And let's not confuse the matter: it's not about our bank accounts — it's about our hearts, our time, our talents, and our treasures. We are to be generous, willing to share, and rich in good deeds for the glory of God.

He promises that blessings follow generosity:

"Command those who are rich in this present world not to be arrogant nor to

put their hope in wealth, which is so uncertain, but to put their hope in God, who richly provides us with everything for our enjoyment. Command them to do good, to be rich in good deeds, and to be generous and willing to share. In this way they will lay up treasure for themselves as a firm foundation for the coming age, so that they may take hold of the life that is truly life."

— *(1 Timothy 6:17–19, NIV)*

There are certain varieties of vegetables that are classified as determinate or indeterminate varieties. The terms differentiate between whether the variety of vegetable will grow to a given size, produce all of its crop within a short period of time, then die down (determinate); or whether it will begin to produce slowly, continuing to grow as a plant and to provide the edible part of the plant over a prolonged period of time (indeterminate).

Recently I planted a determinate variety of tomato, which I don't usually do. But its specific qualities of taste and size sounded wonderful, so I planted it. It started off with a bang, but fizzled before leaving the launching pad. I got three disappointing tomatoes from the plants. Then the plants just stood there, with no tomatoes and no flowers, taking up valuable garden space.

Indeterminate varieties, on the other hand, just keep growing and producing. I sometimes cannot keep up with the harvest and some of the fruit falls to the ground. In a few weeks the fallen tomato seeds start germinating and sending up volunteers. This can give you more plants and a second crop of tomatoes in one season. Again, more abundance.

We can choose which seeds we will sow when we are choosing our variety of tomatoes. Similarly, we can choose the seeds we sow into the kingdom for God:

"Remember this: Whoever sows sparingly will also reap sparingly, and whoever sows generously will also reap generously. Each of you should give what you have decided in your heart to give, not reluctantly or under compulsion, for God loves a cheerful giver. And God is able to bless you abundantly, so that in all things at all times, having all that you need, you will abound in every good work."
— (2 Corinthians 9:6–8, NIV)

Although God tells us to "bring the best of the first fruits of your soil to the house of the Lord your God" (Exodus 34:26, NIV), first fruits are not necessarily the best of the fruit when it comes to growing vegetables. Usually the first vegetables are small and few. As the plant matures and the roots go deeper, taking in more nutrients, the vegetables tend to be bigger and more prolific. I believe that what God meant when he asked us to give our first fruits was to not only give our best but also to give before taking care of ourselves. This is both an act of obedience and an act of faith. When we give our first fruits, we show our Father that we are trusting him for our provision and not relying on ourselves or our own ability.

As we bring our first fruits to the Lord, we have no idea of how or when he will bless that offering. But we can have assurance that he will bless it. And just as an indeterminate plant produces over and over, so God's blessings will be given. As we harvest from an indeterminate plant, the plant is encouraged to produce more and better fruit. Horticulturists teach that with some vegetables or fruits, in order to produce the best quality fruit, it is wise to remove some of the blooms when the plants begin to produce blossoms. This encourages the plant to focus its energy and nutrients on a smaller quantity of fruit production and thereby produce better quality fruit. Think of the expression, "quality is better than quantity." Maybe there are too many blooms in our life. Multitasking is often thought of positively, or as a sign of productivity, but is it really? If you are multitasking, you can sometimes accomplish many things. But are those things meaningful accomplishments or just small, fast fruits that were quickly grown and not fully mature? If we bring a basket of small, low-quality fruit to the altar as an offering, does God look upon it the same as if we bring one high-quality fruit that was produced through an act of care, love, and faithfulness? He searches our hearts and desires. He desires our best, not our quickest. Do one thing excellently rather than many things poorly.

God's blessings are indeterminate. We cannot give more than God gives. I have experienced some years of overproduction in a tomato crop. The plants have produced so long and so many fruit that there were still green tomatoes developing as a frost approached in early fall. The only thing that stops the growth is the change of seasons. Some years have found me so busy that I didn't have time to clean the dead plants from the garden, and so the remaining tomatoes fall onto the soil. In spring volunteer tomato plants grow up from the seeds of last year's unharvested tomatoes. Even in death life springs forth, giving more indeterminate blessings. Unending provision and blessing.

"Bring the whole tithe into the storehouse, that there may be food in my house. Test me in this," says the Lord Almighty, "and see if I will not throw open the floodgates of heaven and pour out so much blessing that there will not be room enough to store it."
—Malachi 3:10 (NIV)

Favorite Recipe

TOO-MANY-TOMATOES SALSA

3–4 ripe tomatoes
1 medium onion
1–2 jalapeno peppers
1 tablespoon minced garlic
Chopped cilantro
Salt to taste

Chop tomatoes and onion to desired size. Dice peppers. Mix together in bowl with remaining ingredients. Serve fresh with tortilla chips.

Notes

Devotion Thirteen

Sharing and Imparting Your Gifts

I want to share a thankful heart with you for your encouragement. If you ever wonder whether you make a difference or can be used by God in your little corner of the world, listen to my story and see that you can change a person's life forever.

Growing Tip from Tim
"Till up the row, plant the seed, and get outta the way!"

July 20, 2013

While digging potatoes today my heart overflowed with gratitude. I was thankful to God for the harvest, but also for a friend. When my husband, Don, and I moved to North Carolina in 2002, we met Tim and Sharon Bushey. Tim had been a dairy farmer in Minnesota for many years and had moved to North Carolina with his wife in the late 90's. They started a small, one-acre farm in North Carolina, just growing food for themselves and for their friends and neighbors. Tim is the kind of farmer who farms because he loves it. Everything about it is a pleasure for him. If he has a bad crop or an insect or any type of obstacle; he calmly researches the problem, tries again, and succeeds. Tim doesn't want to be anything more than what God made him to be. He is content being a blue-collar guy from a humble, New England family. He lives his life quietly and committedly: faithful to God, his wife, and his friends. He is a testament of contentment in every season.

When we moved into our house with four acres, we had no intention of farming. Suburb girl here never grew anything more than a marigold. Tim and Sharon came to dinner one Sunday and said, "You should start growing your own food." I believe my reply was, "Are you crazy! Who the heck wants to do all that work?" But Tim is a great encourager; it is his gift. So the next day he brought over his tiller and tilled up a garden for us.

Don and Tim

The garden looked huge to me, though it was only about 10 x 20 feet. Three years later we were growing half an acre of vegetables, thanks to a friend who taught me more than I could ever share with you all in five years. Tim came to our home countless times and helped us clear and plow the land; he loaded his tractor on his trailer and drove thirty-five minutes to our house when we didn't have a tractor of our own. He taught Don about tractors, and helped him restore an antique David Bradley that we used on our farm. He spent many a Sunday afternoon in our gardens, planting or harvesting with us. Sometimes we would get overwhelmed and he would encourage us to not give up, or

tell us to take things slow. He taught me how to think things through and research, read, and experiment. Those lessons have brought me great success in my gardening.

Tim is a true friend. He is still the person I call when something in my garden looks weird, or when I encounter something new there. God makes us who we are and gives us gifts and talents to be what we are meant to be. But he also sends people into our lives to be encouragement, to be true friends, and to walk alongside us as we walk down the roads of our lives. While harvesting my potatoes today, I was thanking God for the beautiful crop; then I called Tim to share my success with him, because ten years ago I told him he was crazy when we had the following conversation:

"Get yourself fifty pounds of seed potatoes and plant them."
"How many potatoes will we get from fifty pounds?" I said.
"About 250."
I laughed, "What am I gonna do with 250 pounds of potatoes?"
"Eat 'em. Can 'em. Save some for seed, and give some away."

That encouragement ended up changing my life forever. Just Tim being Tim helped turn me from a suburbanite into a homesteader—from eating store-bought, pesticide-filled, and processed food to growing all my own produce organically—who preps for winter and shares the bounty with those who can't grow their own. Don't ever think you can't make a difference in someone's life just by the way you live yours. Share with someone today about your homesteading habits. Give them a potato you grew; then when they say they never tasted a potato so good, tell them they can grow their own too!

July 14, 2015

I wrote this above entry as a Facebook post back in 2013. We had moved away from North Carolina for three years, and during that time we missed our friends deeply. Every time I would work in my tiny 200 square foot garden on the one-eighth-acre yard, I reflected back to our farm days in North Carolina and our friend Tim. When we returned to North Carolina in December of 2013, one of the biggest blessings for us was to be geographically close to Tim and Sharon again. Not that we lost touch with them. We still spoke with them weekly on the phone. And for the three years we lived in Massachusetts Tim, drove 1,200 miles round trip each year to visit and spend a week with us. For my husband Don, Tim was truly closer than a brother. For me he was my farm buddy and mentor. You may have noticed the wording has changed from present tense to past tense. Well that is because on March 30 of this year, Tim went home to be with the Lord he loved. He would say that when he passed he wanted to either go in his sleep or while behind his tractor. God is faithful to those who love him. Tim spent his last weekend visiting and helping us by bringing a load of manure from a local stable with his trailer on Friday, having dinner with us on Saturday, and helped Don do some brake work on his truck on Sunday. On Monday of the following week, he planted his kale for his chickens and hilled up his emerging potato plants. Sometime between Monday evening and Tuesday morning, he woke up in heaven, face-to-face with Jesus. The following week my husband had the honor of spreading Tim's ashes in his garden, and we, his friends, worked him into the soil, where he wished to be to God's glory.

Live life to God's fullest, not your or anyone else's fullest. Our definition of fullest may come with unmet expectations and unfulfilled dreams. I am sure Tim had some of these moments in his life, but he always met them hand-in-hand with God. When we live out our destiny with peace, grace, and faith; we will find contentment in the simple everyday things like sowing seeds, going to our favorite farm-supply store, or sharing Sunday

dinner with friends after helping them plant their new garden. Do not ever think you have nothing to offer others. Your talent, which might seem like no great accomplishment to you, can be a life-changing gift to someone else.

Tim never had children of his own, but he was a father, brother, and uncle to many. He left a wonderful legacy that will continue to be passed on to others for many generations by those who knew him, loved him, and were privileged to call him friend.

>Thank you, Father, for Tim.
>Thank you, Tim. See ya soon, Buddy.

Inspiration in the Garden and the Kitchen

I am an inspired cook. I get most of my inspiration from God. He has kept me company many times in my kitchen, giving me ideas and suggestions on various combinations of flavors, textures, herbs and spices. Since it is God who created all the wonderful foods with which we are provisioned, I consider him the Master Chef.

I am by nature a traditionalist. I was born to parents in their midlife who were grandchildren of Irish and Italian immigrants. I learned from traditional Italian and Irish family life and traditional foods. As in many families around the world, meals brought the family together. My mother did not enjoy cooking, but she was a good cook. Nevertheless, she was not adventurous in her cooking. When you do not enjoy doing something, you tend to not get too adventurous. I spent much of my childhood in the kitchen watching and helping. I loved food from a very young age. Mostly because it meant all my family would be together and I would have time with them. But I also loved the aromas, preparation, and presentation. I am a member of one of the last generations to have had the benefit of home-economics classes offered in the public-school system. I took three years of sewing and three years of cooking. I relished every moment of these classes and excelled in them. It was in school where I acquired my own adventurous spirit for cooking. I loved to bake, something my mother almost never did. If we had desserts in our house, they were store-bought. So my mother loved it as I got older and began baking at home.

All my adult life I have enjoyed cooking. The entire process from shopping to presentation is fun for me. In my kitchen I am adventurous! I love to try new recipes, but I also find returning to my traditional roots. Gardening has made my culinary life even richer. I grow nearly all of our produce, and have found fellow homesteaders to purchase meats from. I also have a small flock of hens to give us our own fresh eggs. God has used the love of gardening he placed in me to inspire me in the kitchen. When I

first started growing vegetables, I only thought to grow the basics: tomatoes, cucumbers, peppers, and green beans. Each spring, however, I had the desire to try other veggies and even berries. Over the years when I see recipes for a particular vegetable that sounds good to me, I will grow that vegetable, adding it to my gardens.

Inspiration comes from many places: tradition, recipes, friends, and, of course, seed catalogs.

So I thought after sharing more about my own gardening and cooking journey with you, I would share some recipes that have become my favorites over the years. And I hope you too will be inspired to try growing a vegetable or fruit that you have never grown before. Then you will get with God in the garden and the kitchen, and see what he inspires you to use that veggie or fruit for. I sometimes even grow a vegetable my husband and I do not like, but we know someone who does. They may not have the ability or space to grow it themselves. Then we surprise them with it, blessing them with that which God has blessed us and sowing seeds of love.

That still small voice can be heard in the garden and even in the kitchen. Be inspired. Be adventurous. Share the bounty. Enjoy the journey. I hope you will try some of my favorite recipes, and then use the blank pages we have provided to create some of your own.

Blessings and happy gardening,
Susan

More of Susan's Inspired Recipes

BROCCOLI CHEDDAR CHEESE SOUP

This soup is easy and quick to put together, especially if you save a step by cooking the broth veggie mixture the day before. Cheesy and delicious, this soup makes a great fall and winter dish when broccoli is starting to be harvested from the cold-weather garden crops.

6 tablespoons unsalted butter
1 small onion, chopped
1/4 cup all-purpose flour
2 cups half-and-half
3 cups low-sodium chicken broth or vegetable broth
1/4 teaspoon freshly grated nutmeg
4 cups broccoli florets (about 1 head)
2 1/2 cups (about 8 ounces) shredded sharp white and yellow cheddar cheese
Salt and pepper to taste

Chop broccoli and onion, and simmer in broth in a large pot till crisp and tender. Cool slightly. Chop or puree broccoli and broth mixture in food processor or mash with a potato masher to desired consistency. Set aside.

In a separate pot, melt butter and add flour, whisking until a paste. Remove from heat. Bring broth mixture to gentle boil, whisk in butter-flour roux. Bring to simmer and simmer until thickened. Add half-and-half, heat through. Add nutmeg, salt, and pepper. Remove pot from heat. Blend in shredded cheese and stir till melted. Serve with crispy French rolls.

BEET SALAD

My husband and I adore beets. They are easy to grow, and in Zones 6–8 you can easily grow two crops, one in early spring and another in mid-fall to early winter. They are incredibly nutritious and delicious. This salad is one of my favorite spring recipes since spinach is abundant in the garden in spring.

Fresh or pickled beets—sliced or chunked
Fresh spinach leaves
Hard-boiled egg
Blue cheese crumbles
Plain or glazed walnuts
Olive oil
Balsamic vinegar

Arrange cleaned, fresh spinach leaves on salad plates. Cut one hard-boiled egg in half or quarters and arrange around outer edges on top of spinach. Arrange beets in a mound in center of spinach bed. Sprinkle blue cheese and walnuts over entire salad. Serve with dressing made of oil and vinegar (2:1).

ZUCCHINI BROWNIES

If you are like me, you are always looking for new ways to use all the zucchini your garden gives. Zucchini bread is wonderful but you and I can only eat so much of it before yawning with boredom. A friend gave me their recipe, and I tweaked it a bit, making it with applesauce for a healthier version. The kids will never know there is a veggie in these brownies.

1/2 cup vegetable oil or applesauce
1 1/4 cup sugar
2 teaspoons vanilla
2 cups all purpose flour
1/2 cup unsweetened cocoa powder
1 1/2 teaspoons baking soda
1 teaspoon salt
2 cups shredded zucchini
1/2 cup chopped walnuts

Frosting:
6 tablespoons unsweetened cocoa
1/4 cup butter
2 cups confectioner's sugar
1/4 cup milk
1/2 teaspoon vanilla extract

Preheat oven to 350°F. Grease and flour a 9 x 13–inch baking pan. In a large bowl, mix together the oil, sugar, and 2 teaspoons vanilla until well blended. Combine the flour, 1/2 cup cocoa, baking soda, and salt; stir into the sugar mixture. Fold in the zucchini and walnuts. Spread evenly into the prepared pan. Bake for 25 to 30 minutes in the preheated oven, until brownies spring back when gently touched.

To make the frosting, melt together the 6 tablespoons of cocoa and butter; set aside to cool. In a medium bowl, blend together the confectioner's sugar, milk, and 1/2 teaspoon vanilla. Stir in the cocoa mixture. Spread over cooled brownies before cutting into squares.

Notes

Notes

Notes

Notes

SUSAN ELANE BERRY

"Build houses and dwell in them; plant gardens and eat their fruit."

—*Jeremiah 29:5 (NKJV)*

About the Author

Susan grew up in the suburbs, twenty minutes south of Boston. At fourteen, when she lost her father, she called out to God. And while it would be another decade before she became a Christian, Susan felt God's hand on her life. Looking back over the years, she knows that God has never left her side.

Susan and her husband, Don, live in North Carolina on a small, half-acre homestead. They have two grown sons and one granddaughter. Susan loves to write, garden, cook, and cuddle with her chickens and her two dogs. At age fifty, Susan began to study horticulture.

Spending time in the garden is a joy for Susan. She sees God in every leaf, baby vegetable, soil particle, and pollinating bee. She loves watching creation flourish beneath her hands, which on a perfect day have lots of dirt on them.

www.ingramcontent.com/pod-product-compliance
Lightning Source LLC
Chambersburg PA
CBHW040330300426
44113CB00020B/2706